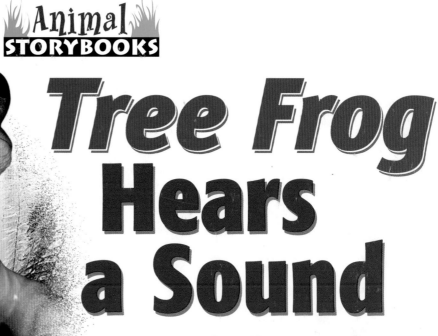

Animal
STORYBOOKS

Tree Frog
Hears
a Sound

Story by Rebecca Johnson
Photos by Steve Parish

GARETH**STEVENS**
GS
PUBLISHING
A Member of the WRC Media Family of Companies

Please visit our web site at: www.garethstevens.com
For a free color catalog describing Gareth Stevens Publishing's list of high-quality books
and multimedia programs, call 1-800-542-2595 (USA) or 1-800-387-3178 (Canada).
Gareth Stevens Publishing's fax: (414) 332-3567.

Library of Congress Cataloging-in-Publication Data

Johnson, Rebecca, 1966–
    [Tree-frog tangles]
    Tree frog hears a sound / story by Rebecca Johnson; photos by Steve Parish. — North American ed.
       p. cm. — (Animal storybooks)
    Summary: A red-eyed tree frog hops through the rain forest in the direction of the most beautiful sound
she has ever heard, meeting various other frogs along the way.
    ISBN 0-8368-5976-6 (lib. bdg.)
    1. Red-eyed tree frog—Juvenile fiction. [1. Tree frogs—Fiction. 2. Frogs—Fiction.] I. Parish, Steve, ill.
II. Title.
PZ10.3.J683Tr   2005
[E]—dc22
                                          2005042630

First published as *Tree-Frog Tangles* in 2002 by Steve Parish Publishing Pty Ltd, Australia.
Text copyright © 2002 by Rebecca Johnson. Photos copyright © 2002 by Steve Parish Publishing.
Series concept by Steve Parish Publishing.

This U.S. edition first published in 2006 by
Gareth Stevens Publishing
A Member of the WRC Media Family of Companies
330 West Olive Street, Suite 100
Milwaukee, Wisconsin 53212 USA

This edition copyright © 2006 by Gareth Stevens, Inc.

Gareth Stevens series editor: Dorothy L. Gibbs
Gareth Stevens cover and title page designs: Dave Kowalski

Printed in the United States of America

1 2 3 4 5 6 7 8 9 09 08 07 06 05

"What was that sound?" wondered the red-eyed tree frog.

She had been sitting on a leaf,
watching a tasty-looking bug,
when she first heard it.

The frog sat very still and listened. But, now, she heard nothing.

5

Hoping to hear
the sound again,
the little frog
climbed to the top
of a tall stick.

But, instead
of hearing
the sound, she
was startled by
a barking noise.

Looking down, she could see that the barking sound was coming from a white-lipped tree frog.

The red-eyed tree frog was
very disappointed. That was
not the sound she wanted to hear.

Just then, she heard the sound again.

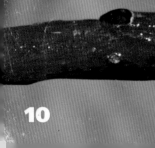

It came
from far away,
and it was the
most beautiful sound
she had ever heard.

The little
red-eyed tree frog
set off to follow
the sound.

She was jumping
from leaf to leaf
so quickly that
she almost fell.

When she heard someone laughing at her, she was very annoyed, until she realized that it was just the call of a Roth's tree frog.

The red-eyed tree frog was so determined to find the sound that she jumped right on top of a big green tree frog.

"Oh! Please, excuse me," she stammered. Then she hopped away.

Racing on through the rain forest
in huge leaps and bounds, she could
hear the calls of a bleating tree frog
growing louder and louder.

But she wanted to hear
the sound — the lovely,
lovely sound.

"I must be getting closer," she thought to herself.

Then, she heard it! Softly, at first . . .

. . . now louder!

She looked down.
Just below her was
the handsomest frog
she had ever seen.

He was sitting
on a beautiful flower,
singing just for her.

23

Now she hears
his lovely sound
every day.